FOR LADIES CLASSES

GLORIFYING GOD

(Revised Edition)

By Mrs. W. R. Smith

Published By
BIBLICAL RESEARCH PRESS
774 East North 15th Street
Abilene, Texas
79601

GLORIFYING GOD

By Mrs. W. R. Smith
(Revised Edition)

BIBLICAL RESEARCH PRESS,
ABILENE, TEXAS

Library of Congress Catalog Card No. 79 87465
ISBN–0-89112-134-X

Printed in the United States of America

TABLE OF CONTENTS

GLORIFYING GOD

INTRODUCTION

Purpose: (1) To give brief prospectus of the lessons to follow; (2) To create in each a desire to learn how to glorify God.

God puts us in this world for one purpose and our aim in life should be to fulfill that purpose, namely, *TO GLORIFY GOD.*

Notice I Cor. 10:31; 6:19-20; 1:31; Matt. 5:16; I Pet. 2:11-12, 4:11; Rev. 14:7; Jno. 15:8. Find others. The heavens declare the glory of God and the angels give thanks, honor and glory unto Him. Shall man alone be ungrateful?

1. *What is it to glorify God?* "It is the bringing into prominence of His attitudes, the working out of His purposes." Jesus glorified God by doing His will. We can do the same. Jno. 17:4-10. Those who glorify Him act as redeemed children in all *relationships* of life. I Cor. 10:31.

2. *Why glorify God?*
   a. It is commanded.
   b. A satisfaction of knowing we are pleasing God.
   c. A grateful acknowledgment of God's goodness.
   d. It is the only way to secure our own highest happiness.
   e. Remember the danger in any other life style (Examples: Acts 12:20-23; Dan. 5:18-23; Rev. 16:9).

3. *To what does it apply?* Everything. "No interest in life is so wide, no relationship so sacred, no occupation so honorable as not to come under this principle." Then nothing we do is insignificant, but everything we do is of supreme significance because of I Cor. 10:31. The commonest things must be done with the highest motive and our greatest deeds must escape a low or selfish motive. Notice I Cor. 10:31; Acts 5:1-10; Num. 20:11-12.

4. *What does it involve?*
   a. Conversion. Rom. 8:5-17; Eph. 3:21. We cannot live to the glory of God if we have not accepted Christ as our Savior, therefore we must be converted before we can glorify Him, Phil. 2:11, II Thess. 1:10-12.
   b. *Direct service to God in worship.* Psa. 50:23; Jno. 4: 22-24.
   c. *Duties to ourselves.* By self-improving, II Pet. 3:18; Jno. 15:8; by increase in physical, mental and spiritual health, I Pet. 2:1-2 I Cor. 6:13-19; II Pet. 1:5, 3:18.
   d. *Duties to others.* When we truly serve men, we serve God. We can glorify God by seeking to advance interests of our fellowman. Matt. 22:37-39; 7:12 I Cor. 10: 23, 24, 28-33; Heb. 10:24. The person who holds the supreme purpose–to Glorify God–will be found the kindest, most generous and most helpful man by all his fellowmen. He will not offend the conscience of his fellowman, nor cause him to stumble but will love him, forgive him, earnestly seek his salvation, and be willing to practice self-denial that the life may be pleasing unto Him, II Cor. 5:9-10.

REVIEW QUESTIONS

1. Memorize I Cor. 10:31.

2. What do you mean when you say, "That child brings glory and honor to his parents"? Now, what does it mean for one to glorify God?

3. What part of one's life is to be a glory to God? How much is left out? Evaluate the expression, "*Whatsoever* ye do, do *all* to the glory of God."

4. Do the children of the Jones family bring honor or dishonor to the parents in the Smith family? Now, who is it that brings honor to God? Show why the first unit (lesson two and three) would naturally be on the subject of how to become a child of God.

5. Show how the next unit (lessons four through nine) naturally follow unit one.

6. The remaining lessons are practical lessons on living the Christian life so as to fulfill our AIM IN LIFE–TO GLORIFY GOD.
   a. What are the duties to ourselves?
   b. What are our duties to others?

Lesson I

HOW ARE WE SAVED?

Purpose: (1) To show how a person glorifies God through the first steps of obedience;

(2) To show the proper relationships of all personalities and things which are involved in the salvation of mankind;

(3) To give a fuller and a deeper appreciation of the plan of salvation.

Introduction: Noah, a preacher of righteousness, II Pet. 2:5, was saved by faith, ark, Heb. 11:7, and water, I Pet. 3:20. How?

I. Salvation is ascribed to:

A. God, Rom. 6:23; I Tim. 4:10. . . . . A. Grace, Eph. 2:8

B. Christ, Matt. 1:21 I Tim. 1:15 . . . . B. Blood, I Jno. 1:7; Rom. 5:9, 10

C. Holy Spirit, Rom. 1:16; I Pet. 1:12. . . . . C. Gospel, I Cor. 15:1, 2

D. Apostles, Acts 26:16-18 . . . . D. Preaching, I Cor. 1:21

E. Ourselves, Acts 2:40; Phil. 2:12 . . . . E. Faith, Jno. 3:16 Acts 16:31; Heb. 11:6; Jas. 2:22

Repentance, Lk. 13:3; Acts 3:19; II Cor. 7:10

Confession, Matt. 10:32
Rom. 10:10
Baptism, Mk. 16:16;
I Pet. 3:20, 21
Works, Phil. 2:12;
Jas. 2:24
Hope, Rom. 8:24, 25

F. Others, I Tim. 4:16

II. How are we saved by so many persons and things?
A. *Grace* caused God to devise the plan of salvation.
B. *Christ's Blood* is the meritorious cause.
C. The *gospel,* revealed by the *Holy Spirit,* is the plan.
D. The *preaching* of the *Apostles* made the plan known to mankind.
E. *Faith* is that which enables *us* to accept the gospel.
F. *Repentance* causes *us* to turn from sin unto God.
G. *Confession* is *our* vow of allegiance to God.
H. *Baptism* puts *us* into Christ.
I. *Works* and *Hope* continue *our* preparation for Heaven.

Conclusion: This has been God's plan of saving people since the first Pentecost after Christ's Resurrection, therefore note Gal. 1:8, 9 and Rev: 22:14.

REVIEW QUESTIONS

1. Memorize Prov. 14:12 and Matt. 7:13, 14. This lesson is not the way that "seemeth right" but the "narrow way" that IS RIGHT.

2. Show how Noah was saved by faith, the ark and water. Which one, if any, could have been left out? Explain the part each had in his salvation. Which things were to be done as Noah's part; as God's part?

3. Read scriptures showing all the THINGS that are involved in the salvation of mankind.

4. Read scriptures showing all the *Persons* that are involved in the salvation of mankind.

5. What relationship do you see between the PERSONS in the left column and the THINGS in the right column?

6. Evaluate the statement, "What man cannot do for himself, God does for him; that which man can do for himself, God expects him to do." Apply this principle to the list on the lesson sheet.

7. Study carefully each step under "II," showing the essential value of each step.

8. What is the thought in Gal. 1:8, 9 and Rev. 22:14?

9. God has done His part. Have you glorified God in your obedience to that which is your part? If so, are you making any effort toward getting others to do the same thing?

10. Quote I Cor. 10:31b—"Whatsoever ye . . ." therefore ye eat or drank or whatsoever ye do do all to the glory of God,

Lesson II

THE GOSPEL

Purpose: (1) To learn what the gospel is and how to obey it; (2) To encourage all who have not obeyed the gospel to do so that they may glorify God.

Introduction: The gospel includes:

1. *Facts* to be believed: works, death, burial, and resurrection of Christ. (See I Cor. 15:1-4.)
2. *Commandments* to be obeyed: faith, repentance, confession, baptism.
3. *Promises* to be enjoyed: remission of sins, gifts of the Spirit, eternal life.

I. The Gospel:

A. *What is it?* I Cor. 15:1-4; Acts 2:22-24, 30-32, 36: The works, death, burial, and resurrection of the Lord Jesus Christ.

B. *What must man do?* II Thess. 1:6-10: Obey it!

C. *How?* Romans 6:17: A form or likeness of the death, burial, and resurrection of Christ; Romans 6:1-9: (a) "dead with Christ," vs. 8; (b) "Burial with him by baptism unto death," vs 4; (c) "United together in the likeness of his death, we shall be also in the likeness of his resurrection," vs 5.

D. Results: 1. A change of masters, Rom. 6:16-22.
2. A change from wages to reward, Rom. 6:23.

II. Examples of New Testament Conversions:

Acts 2:14-41 Pentecostians	Heard	Believed	Repented	Baptized	1. Remission of sins 2. Gift of Holy Spirit

Acts 8:5-12 Samaritans	Heard	Believed			Baptized	
Acts 8:26-39 Eunuch	Heard	Believed		Confessed	Baptized	
Acts 9:1-18 Saul	Heard				Baptized	Wash away sins
Acts 10:1-48 Cornelius	Heard				Baptized	
Acts 16:13-15 Lydia	Heard				Baptized	
Acts 16:25-34 Jailer	Heard	Believed			Baptized	Thou shalt be saved
Acts 18:8 Corinthians	Heard	Believed			Baptized	
Conclusion:	Heard	Believed	Repented	Confessed	Baptized	1. Remission of sins 2. Gift of Holy Spirit 3. Saved–eternal life

III. Notice: Heb. 11:6; Lk. 13:3; Matt. 10:32; I Pet. 3:20, 21.

Conclusion:
1. This gospel came from heaven, Gal. 1:11, 12; II Tim. 2:2.
2. We are accursed if we preach another gospel, Gal. 1:6-9.

REVIEW QUESTIONS

1. What is the gospel?

2. What must man do with it? What will be the result if he does not?

3. How can man obey a "form of doctrine"? Point out specific words which show a likeness to Christ's DEATH, BURIAL, and RESURRECTION. What is the significance of "buried by baptism into death"?

4. What changes are brought about as a result of turning from a life of sin to a life of righteousness?

5. Study each of the cases of conversion recorded in Acts–(assign each to an individual who tells the incident in his own words). What is the conclusion? If we hear the same thing, believe the same thing, and do the same thing, can we expect the same blessings?

6. Study "III" until you can quote each one from memory, giving book, chapter and verse. Why should all be able to do this?

7. From where did the gospel preached by the apostles come? What is the result if I change it?

8. Is this the gospel you heard, believed, and obeyed?

9. Review:

My aim in life must be . . . . This is done only . . . . (II Thess. 1:10; Eph. 3:20, 21), therefore my first step should be to become a . . . . God's . . . . caused him to send . . . . into the world who paid the penalty of sin by . . . . The Holy Spirit revealed the . . . . to the . . . . who . . . . and recorded it for mankind. Our part now is to . . . .
When we have done this we may expect such blessings as . . . . From this time on our every act should be . . . . (I Cor. 10:31).

Lesson III

GLORIFYING GOD IN WORSHIP

Purpose: (1) To learn what constitutes worship;
(2) To warn against perverting the God-given worship which is the only true worship.

Introduction:

A. Meaning of worship: to respect, to honor, to revere, an earnest homage done to one in authority.—Webster

B. Principles governing New Testament worship, Matt. 28:18; Jno. 4:24.

C. Perverted worship: Ezek. 22:26; Lev. 10-1-10; Matt. 15:9; Acts 17:23; Col. 2:22, 23.

I. Old and New Testament worship contrasted:

A. The Day: Ex. 35:1-3—Rev. 1:10; Acts 20:7. Notice Gal. 5:1-4.

B. The Spirit: Lev. 1-27 (ceremonial and ritualistic)—Jno. 4:24; I Cor. 14:15; Eph. 5:19; Col. 3:16.

C. Place: Ex. 25:8, 9, 22; Deut. 12:10-13, 32—Jno. 4:20-26; Mk. 16:15.

D. Acts of worship:

1. *Preaching or teaching God's Word:* Deut. 6:4-7; 11:19—Acts 2:42; 20:7; Mk. 16:15.
2. *Music:* Psa. 150; 33:2, 3 (no record of any instruments in the Holy Place, which was a pattern of the church, Heb. 8:4-6; See also Col. 3:16; Eph. 5:19.
3. *Prayer:* Children of God have always prayed to their Heavenly Father. In the New Testament prayers are "in Christ's name," Jno. 14:13, 14; Col. 3:17.

4. *Fellowship or giving:* Lev. 27:31, 32–Acts 2:42; II Cor. 9:6, 7.
5. *Lord's Supper:* Lev. 24:5-8–Acts 20:7; I Cor. 11:23-26; 11:34.

II. Results if changed:

A. Old Testament example, Lev. 10:1-10.
B. New Testament, II Jno. 9.

Conclusion: If the God-given worship is observed, then God is glorified. I Cor. 10:31.

REVIEW QUESTIONS

God has a right to make laws, fulfill them or abolish them. What was right for Jewish people to observe is not right for the Christians unless given to the Christian. Why?

Examples: Jewish laws of incense, animal sacrifices, etc., are not for the Christian; neither instruments of music, for we are to "make melody in the heart" (Eph. 5:19). A LACK OF AUTHORITY IN ANYTHING RELIGIOUS IS GROUNDS ENOUGH FOR NOT HAVING IT.

1. What is the meaning of worship?

2. Of what significance are Matt. 28:18 and Jno. 4:24 in the study of worshipping God? Does it make any difference how we worship God?

3. What is the difference in common matters and holy matters? Give examples. Give examples of perverted worship and the penalty for such. Evaluate the statement: "A lack of authority in anything religious is grounds enough for not using it."

4. Who controls the home? the state? the church? Explain why it would be sinful to use a thing in a religious service and not sinful to use that same thing in the home or state.

5. Discuss the New Testament worship as to the day, the spirit, and the acts engaged in as worship. Contrast this with worship of Old Testament times.

6. If these are changed, what will be the result?

7. Quote I Cor. 10:31.

Lesson IV

WORSHIP: PRAYER

Purpose: (1) To learn what the Bible teaches concerning acceptable prayer;
(2) To help each one to appreciate more fully this privilege;
(3) To encourage each one to be more dependent upon the Father and to give Him the glory for all blessings.

Introduction: Prayer should never be a formality, but an earnest expression from the heart. I Jno. 3:2. "Now we are the sons of God," therefore, we can go to the *Father* as His child and ask for our needs and express our thanks for what we have received. Notice:
Rom. 8:32–freely gives us all things.
Matt. 7:11–give to them that ask.
Phil. 4:6–let your request be made known.
Heb. 4:15 and Rom. 8:26, 27–Christ and Holy Spirit understand and intercede for us.

I. Pray:

A. Who? Jno. 9:31; I Pet. 3:12; I Jno. 3:22; Prov. 28:9.
B. How? Rom. 8:26, 27–know not how
Jas. 1:6, 7; Mk. 11:24 }ask in faith
Mk. 11:25, 26; Mt. 6:14, 15 } forgiving heart
Jas. 4:3–unselfish
Lk. 18:10-14–in humility
Jno. 14:13, 14–in Christ's name
C. What? Jas. 1:5–wisdom;

Heb. 4:15, 16–mercy and grace to help in time of need
Jas. 5:15–for sick
Jas. 5:16a–for one another
Matt. 26:41–not enter into temptation
II Thess. 3:1, 2 } spread of the gospel
Col. 4:3 }
Acts 8:22–forgiveness
I Tim. 2:1, 2–all men
I Jno. 5:14, 15–for anything

D. Why? Jas. 5:16b; Phil. 4:6, 7–prayer changes things.

Conclusion: God will answer prayers but it may not be as we expect, for he is governed by Rom. 8:28.

"He asked for strength that he might achieve;
He was made weak that he might obey.
He asked for health that he might do greater things;
He was given infirmity that he might do better things.
He asked for riches that he might be happy;
He was given poverty that he might be wise,
He asked for power that he might have the praise of men;
He was given weakness that he might feel the need of God.
He asked for all things that he might enjoy life;
He was given life that he might enjoy all things."

–Doran

REVIEW QUESTIONS

1. Discuss the relationship that exists between God and a Christian.

2. Quote scriptures that encourage a child of God to pray.

3. Describe the person whom God has promised to hear.

4. Discuss the significance and meaning of each scripture listed under "B." How?

5. For what can a Christian pray?

6. God knows what we need even before we ask Him, Matt. 6:8; then why pray?

7. What comforting promise do we have when our prayers are answered in a different way from that which we expected?

Lesson V

MUSIC IN NEW TESTAMENT WORSHIP

Purpose: To learn what music is authorized in New Testament worship and to learn how God is to be glorified in this part of the worship.

Introduction: Keep in mind the teachings of Rom. 6:15, Matt. 28:18, Jno. 16:13; II Tim. 3:16, 17 and II Jno. 9.

I. Music of New Testament–that which Christ authorized and the apostles used as they were guided by the Holy Spirit:

   A. Eph. 5:19–"Speaking"–"singing"–"make melody in your heart"
   B. Col. 3:16–"Teaching and admonishing"–"singing with grace in your hearts"
   C. I Cor. 14:15–"Sing"

II. Singing which God approves:

   A. The authorized music: vocal, not instrumental, Eph. 5:19; Col. 3:16.
   B. The authorized kind of songs: Psalms, hymns, and spiritual songs, Eph. 5:19; Col. 3:16.
   C. The authorized motive in singing: Jas. 5:13; Heb. 13:15; Rom. 15:9; Eph. 5:19; Col. 3:16.
      (1) "Praise and thanksgiving unto God."
      (2) "Speaking to yourselves."
      (3) "Teaching and admonishing one another."
   D. How: Acts 16:25; Col. 3:16; Eph. 5:19; I Cor. 14:15; unto God, with the spirit and with the understanding.

Conclusion: Christians should make their singing an outburst of such feelings as adoration, devotion, reverence, petitions, etc. "Be filled with the Spirit–sing and make melody in your heart." Notice Heb. 12:28, 29; I Cor. 10:31.

REVIEW QUESTIONS

1. Firmly fix in your mind the teachings of the scriptures listed in the introduction.
2. Music may be instrumental or vocal. What kind of music did God authorize to be used in the worship described in the New Testament?
3. Describe a person who sings and does not worship. Describe one who worships in song.
4. What warning have we in II Jno. 9? Then why cannot Christians use instruments in their worship?
5. Study the songs in your book. Are they scriptural songs? Which ones can you sing with the Spirit and with the understanding? Which ones would have to be left off? Why?
6. What thoughts are expressed in Heb. 12:28, 29 and I Cor. 10:31?

Lesson VI

WORSHIP: THE LORD'S SUPPER

Purpose: (1) To learn how to partake of the Lord's Supper so as to be pleasing to God, therefore glorifying Him;
(2) To warn against dishonoring God in this act of worship.

Introduction: Notice the Bible expression used: I Cor. 10: 16; 10: 21; 11:20.

I. Worship: The Lord's Supper.

A. Authority:
1. Delivered unto the apostles by Christ. Matt. 26: 26-29.
2. Practice of the early church which was set in order by the apostles who were guided by the Holy Spirit, Acts 2:42, 20:7.
3. Paul recognized it as a part of the worship, I Cor. 11: 23-30.

B. Where observed: Lk. 22:29, 30; I Cor. 11:18-30 (notice vs. 18, 22).

C. When observed: Acts 2:42; 20-7.

D. What was used: Matt. 26: 26-29.

E. Why observe the Lord's Supper:
1. I Cor. 11:24, 25—"in remembrance of me," a memorial—retrospective.
2. I Cor. 11:26—"till I come," anticipation and hope —prospective.
3. I Cor. 11:29, 30—to maintain spiritual vigor.
4. I Cor. 10:17—"We being many are one bread, one body"—fellowship.

5. I Cor. 11:26–"proclaim his death."

F. How to observe the Lord's Supper;

1. I Cor. 11:28–Examine self, prove self, test self:
   (a) As to acceptability of worship, Matt. 5:22-24.
   (b) As to his submissive spirit, and in loving remembrance of Christ, I Cor. 11:24, 25.
2. I Cor. 11:27-29–worthily:
   (a) Though we may be *unworthy*, we may still eat *worthily*, that is, in a prayerful, reverent, repentant spirit; keeping in mind what it memorializes.

   (b) Notice Heb. 10:29-31.

II. "The Importance of the Lord's Supper."
The "Christian who deliberately absents himself from the Lord's Supper on any Lord's Day–

A. Deliberately ignores a command of God, Christ, and the Spirit. I Cor. 11:24, 25.

B. Brands himself or herself a sinner, because he has transgressed Christ's law, and "sin is transgression of the law" (I Jno. 3, 4). "He that knoweth to do good and doeth it not, to him it is sin" (Jas. 4:17).

C. Refuses to "remember Christ." If you say that you can remember Him in other ways or in the Supper at another time, please remember that He said: "Do this."

REVIEW QUESTIONS

1. What other scriptural names may be used when speaking of the Lord's Supper?

2. By what authority do Christians partake of the Lord's Supper?

3. Where is the Lord's Supper to be eaten? Of what does it consist? Does this exclude everything else? When is it to be eaten? How often?

4. Why did God want us to eat the Lord's Supper as an act of worship?

5. Discuss the manner of eating. What is the difference in "being worthy to eat" and "eating worthily"? How may a person eat unworthily?

6. Read carefully section "II." Comment.

7. Quote I Cor. 10:31.

Lesson VII

WORSHIP: GIVING

Purpose: (1) To learn how to give as to glorify God;
(2) To arouse interest in the need;
(3) To encourage each to give so the church will not be handicapped in its work.

Introduction: Parents cannot obey God for their children in the matter of giving any more than they can be baptized for them. We need to learn that a portion of that which is ours (even if given to us) should be given to the Lord.

1. Notice that we are stewards, Lk. 16:10-13; I Pet. 4:10; I Cor. 4:1, 2; Jas. 1:17.
2. Paul exhorted Corinthians to be liberal, II Cor. 8; II Cor. 8:1-24.

I. Giving:

A. Why?

1. It is a means of glorifying God, II Cor. 9:12-15.
2. It is a mark of true religion, I Jno. 3:17-18.
3. We must give an account of what we have, Lk. 19:13-27.
4. It is a way to be blessed or happy, Acts 20:35.
5. It is a means of laying up treasures in heaven. I Tim. 6:17-19; Matt. 6:19-21.
6. God is able to make all material things abound to His children who invest a portion of their earnings in His work, II Cor. 9:6-11; Phil. 4:14-20.
7. Fellowship is an example of the early Christians, Acts 2:42.
8. It is the means of carrying on the Lord's work,

Rom. 12:13; Gal. 2:10; I Tim. 5:16; Mk. 16:15.

B. How?
   1. Give self first, II Cor. 8:5; Rom. 12:1; Rom. 6:13.
   2. Proportionately, I Cor. 16:2; II Cor. 8:12-14.
   3. Not accidentally, but purposefully., II Cor. 9:7.
   4. Voluntarily, II Cor. 9:7.
   5. Cheerfully, II Cor. 9:7.
   6. Bountifully, not sparingly, II Cor. 9:6.
   7. Confidently, II Cor. 9:8-11; Matt. 6:33.
   8. With simplicity, without show, Rom. 12:8; Matt. 6:3, 4.
   9. In Christ's name, Col. 3:17; Mark 9:41.

C. Example of a special contribution, I Cor. 16:2.

Conclusion: God has given the plan. It is the obligation of the individual Christian to put the plan into operation. If God's plan were followed in all congregations, there would be no lack of funds for all our needs.

REVIEW QUESTIONS

1. Is giving as an act of worship a Christian duty or a privilege?

2. Discuss eight reasons why Christians should give. Most will agree with these reasons unless it be "5" and "6." Do you believe these too?

3. Name nine things to be considered if we are to give scripturally—pleasing to God and thereby glorifying Him?

4. Why has God not required a certain amount?

5. If this month I receive $30 per week and contribute $1 and next month I receive $50 per week and contribute $1, what principle has been violated? If I decide to give one-fifth or one-eighth, or one-tenth of my income, regardless of what it is, have I given proportionately or purposefully?

6. What method would you suggest for a Christian to observe who wishes to glorify God in his giving?

7. Quote I Cor. 10:31b.

Lesson VIII

WOMEN TEACHERS OF GOD'S WORD

Purpose: (1) To learn what part women have in teaching God's Word;
(2) To inspire each to be a Christian woman who is a glory to God.

Introduction: Women taught by the authority of God in both Old and New Covenant times. Examples: Miriam, Ex. 15:20; Deborah, Judges 4:4; Huldah, II Chron. 34:22-28; Anna, Lk. 2:36; Priscilla, Acts 18:24-26; Philip's four daughters, Act. 21:9.

I. Teach:

A. Teach aged women to be: (Titus 2:3-8)
1. Holy–"reverent in demeanor." "The movement of the body, the expression of the countenance, what is said, and what is left unsaid–the whole habit and composition or structure of mind and body is to be what becomes a holy woman–all included in the Greek word."–Jerome.
2. True–"not slanderous"–Being kind, soft and loving in her speech.
3. Temperate–"not given to much wine." The habits and usages of the social life are pure.
4. Useful–"teachers of good things"–the right use of the tongue.

B. Teach young women to be:
1. Homekeepers–"love their husbands, love their children, workers at home." First duty of a Christian woman is to make a happy home, which

is impossible without a love for husband and children. Love of husband is her source of strength; love of children is the guarantee of their happiness and welfare. A worthy loving wife (1) is a blessing to her husband, Prov. 12:4; 18:22; (2) brings him honor, Prov. 31:28, 29. Workers at home: (1) Religion gains no honor when home duties are neglected; (2) the husband's interests are preserved by the wife's industry at home; (3) gadding about gets one mixed up in other people's business and tends to spread evil.

2. "Discreet or soberminded"—not a rash or impulsive conduct.
3. "Chaste"—in act, speech, thought and dress.
4. "Kind or good."
5. Obedient—"in subjection to their own husbands." In so doing we become types of the church's submission to Christ and recommend the gospel to unbelieving husbands.

II. Restrictions laid on women teachers:

A. 1 Tim. 2:11, 12—
   1. Learn in quietness,
   2. not to teach over man,
   3. not to usurp authority over man.

B. From the beginning woman has been in subjection to man because (1) she was Adam's helper. I Tim. 2:13; and (2) she, "being deceived, was in the transgression." I Tim. 2:14. Notice Gen. 3:16; I Pet. 3:1; Col. 3:18; Eph. 5:22-24; I Cor. 11:3.

C. How usurp authority over man?
   1. Teach without approval or authority of elders.
   2. Refuse to recognize the headship of husbands in the family.
   3. Refuse to be in subjection to man.
   4. Dominate man—any action which proves she does not recognize the place God has given her.

Conclusion: Paul's admonition to all, Titus 2:11-14.

REVIEW QUESTIONS

1. Give examples of women teachers in Old and New Covenant.

2. What are aged women to be taught? Explain each point.

3. What are young women to be taught? Explain each point.

4. When women do not learn these things, what is the result?

5. What restrictions did God put upon women teachers? Why?

6. How does woman usurp authority over man?

7. Read Paul's admonition to all.

Lesson IX

CHRISTIAN GROWTH

Purpose: (1) To inspire each to grow and bear fruit to the glory of God;
(2) To warn against a lack of growing. Jno. 15:4-8; Eph. 4:11-16; II Pet. 3:18.

Introduction: Some one has well said, "Just as the bud that does not become a flower is a failure so the Christian that does not grow is a failure." Unless the lamp is refilled with oil, it will go out; so it is with the Christian that does not grow. His good works become less frequent, less sincere and less lovely. He deteriorates.

I. Principles of spiritual growth:

A. Desire to grow, I Pet. 2:2; Cf. I Cor. 3:2.
B. Removal of hindrances or harmful habits, Heb. 12:1; I Pet. 2:1, 2; Eph. 4:25:32.
   1. Hindrances in personal life, I Pet. 2:1; (Contrast with I Cor. 13:4 ff):
      a. Malice (notice I Cor. 14:20)
      b. Guile—spirit of deceit.
      c. Hypocrisies—guile manifested.
      d. Envies—pining on the good estate of others.
      e. Evil speaking—envy manifested.
      f. Worldly pleasures }
      g. Cares of the world } Parable of the Soils.
      h. Unholy ambitions }
      i. Love of money
      j. Prejudices
   2. Hindrances in environment:
      a. Go to a place where it is difficult or nearly

impossible to be a Christian.

b. Associations which are a source of great temptation.

3. Hindrances in the local church:
   a. Strife
   b. Division
   c. Self-satisfied
   d. Destructive criticism

C. Partaking of spiritual food: I Pet. 2:2; I Cor. 3:2.

1. Study, II Tim. 2:15. The word of God is the germ of all spiritual life. The word builds up, Acts 20:32; Psa. 1:1-3. Are you growing through study?

2. Prayer, Col. 4:2. As the Christian communes with God, he becomes like God. Growth in piety and in power are not possible without the spirit of grace and supplication. Are *you* using this means to grow?

3. Worship, Rev. 22:9c, including all the activities of true worship. We become assimilated to the character of the object we worship. *Is your worship such as to cause you to grow?*

D. Spiritual exercise: Putting into practice that which is learned, I Tim. 4:7; Heb. 12:1.

1. Jas. 1:21-27, Notice "putting away," "receive word," and "be a doer."
2. II Pet. 1:5-11, vs. 10, "do." Notice results in 10c and 11a.
3. Matt. 25:14-30.
   a. Those who did *something* were rewarded.
   b. He who *did* nothing lost that which he had.
4. Results, Matt. 7:19; Jno. 15:2.

Conclusion: A child checked in development is a freak, a dwarf. Are you a spiritual dwarf? Growth is a sure proof of a healthy life. Where there is no spiritual growth, there is no spiritual life.

REVIEW QUESTIONS

1. Read carefully the introduction.

2. What is necessary for one to grow physically? Apply this to spiritual growth.

3. Examine a tree, vine or bush and notice where the fruit, flowers, etc., grow. Apply this to spiritual growth.

4. Examine carefully Jno. 15:4-8 and II Pet. 3:18.

5. Show how Jas. 1:21-27 sets forth all the principles of growth.

6. What is emphasized in II Pet. 1:10 and Matt. 25:14-30.

7. Read carefully Matt. 7:17-19; Jno. 15:2.

8. Quote Jno. 15:8; II Cor. 10:31b.

Lesson X

GOOD WORKS

Purpose: To encourage each to carry out the command to do good works which glorify God, and to suggest some good works that a Christian woman may do.

Introduction: Purity, meekness, patience, etc., are excellent graces, but are not sufficient justification for our existence. The great end of being is the doing of positive good–good works which glorify God, Matt. 5:16.

I. To do good we must be good, Matt. 12:35; 7:17, 18.

II. Christians are created for good works, Eph. 2:10.

III. "Let us do good," Gal. 6:10; Titus 3:14; Heb. 10:24; 13:16–the duty commanded. "The barren tree is hurtful because it cumbers the ground and draws to itself the fertilizing qualities of the earth, which would make a better tree more fruitful," therefore a man is not harmless who does no good. Only those who DO GOOD are pleasing to God.

IV. "As we have opportunity," Gal. 6:10–the duty bounded by opportunity. Lost opportunities can never be recalled.

V. "Do good to all men and especially to them of the household of faith," Gal. 6:10–the duty is to all within the range of opportunity. We are to do good first to the household of faith on the same principle that we are to remember first the wants of our family.

VI. "Overcome evil with good," Rom. 12:20, 21. The best

way to drive out evil thoughts and evil acts is to busy yourself in good works. Unkindness can be overcome by doing kindness.

VII. Good works for Christian women:

A. Faithful at worship, Heb. 10:24, 25.
B. Rule the household, I Tim. 5:14.
C. Teach, Titus 2:3-5.
D. Visit, Jas. 1:27.
E. Care for the aged, I Tim. 5:4.
F. Hospitality given and refused, II Jno. 10, 11; III Jno. 5, 8.
G. Many works for woman, Prov. 31:10-31.
H. Specific suggestions for each day of the week:

1. Give special attention to an orphan child. Write him Bible stories and other informational stories; remember him on special occasions.
2. Teach a class; attend a class; keep children while another attends a class.
3. Visit hospitals, taking good reading material, flowers, etc., to the patients.
4. Visit the shut-ins (at home, at the old folks home, at the jails, etc.), or send them cards, papers, etc.
5. Visit the sick of the community, doing those things needed.
6. Do a kind deed for a personal enemy or for one whom you know is unfriendly to the church.
7. "Worship in spirit and in truth" each Lord's Day. Suggest other activities.

Conclusion: Select some of these and faithfully do them. Do all of them "as you have opportunity." I Cor. 10:31b; Matt. 5:16.

REVIEW QUESTIONS

1. Memorize Matt. 5:16.

2. What is the first requirement for doing good?

3. We make a machine or some other thing to do a certain work for us. We were created by God for what purpose?

4. Discuss each section of Gal. 6:10.

5. When we obey Gal. 6:10, we have the satisfaction of knowing that we are obeying a command of God. What other advantage is there in doing good. Rom. 12:20, 21.

6. Name and discuss the many good works.

7. I Cor. 10:31b.

Lesson XI

CAREFUL USE OF OPPORTUNITIES

Purpose: To show the necessity of making use of opportunities.

Introduction: The Parable of the Talents impresses upon us the method of making preparation for heaven. We must make use of all our opportunities or suffer the doom of the wicked and lazy servant.

I. The Talents: Matt. 25:14-30

A. The Master . . . . Lord Jesus Christ
B. Servants . . . . Members of visible church
C. Goods. . . . . Spiritual powers and capacities, all means of usefulness
D. Talents . . . . Opportunities for service
E. Going away of the Lord . . . . Withdrawl of Christ from the earth
F. Return of the Lord. . . . . Second coming of Christ
G. Trading of the servants with the talents . . . . . Faithful use of opportunities, capabilities
H. Treatment of servants by their master . . . . . Principles on which the awards will be made.

II. Lessons:

A. In the kingdom there is a diversity which exists among individuals in the matter of opportunities of service. Each is given all he can use and then we are responsible for their use, Matt. 25:15.
B. Opportunities come to us with our improvement of those which we already have. The reward for service is more service. Notice Matt. 13:12; 25:28, 29.

C. When Christ comes, he will take account of every man's work–the fidelity with which his work has been administered. Notice Rom. 14:10-12; II Cor. 5:10; Matt. 25:19.

D. To do nothing at all, when we can do something, is one way of doing wrong, Matt. 25:26-28.

E. Because we do not have big opportunities to do great things is no excuse for not taking advantage of smaller ones.

F. The faithful servants were equally rewarded but the wicked and lazy servant received a two-fold doom, namely, (1) opportunities forfeited and (2) cast out–lost. Matt. 25:30.

Conclusion: How am I using my opportunities? I Cor. 10:31b.

REVIEW QUESTIONS

1. Read the parable and fix clearly in mind what is represented.

2. Upon what basis is each Christian given opportunities for service?

3. Evaluate the statement that reward for service is more service.

4. Ask yourself: "Am I ready and willing for God to take account of my work?"

5. Is "D" under "II" a sin of omission? Is this dangerous too?

6. According to this parable, how does a person get the opportunity to do big things?

7. Contrast the rewards of the servants in the parable. Make the application.

8. Ask yourself these questions:

   A. Do I have the ability to teach others? If so, do I use the opportunity or do I push it aside for others to do?
   B. Am I especially good in doing personal work? If so, am I using every opportunity to do it?
   C. Is my natural ability that of caring for the sick or of making newcomers welcome or interesting people in Bible study? If your means of usefulness is any one of these or some other not named, are you using your opportunities to the fullest? If not, why not? II Cor. 5:10.

9. Read I Cor. 10:31b, I Pet. 4:7-11, 17, 18.

Lesson XII

"THANKSGIVING TO ABOUND UNTO THE GLORY OF GOD"

Purpose: (1) To make each realize more fully the blessings that can be enjoyed by a child of God;
(2) To urge each to give thanks unto the glory of God.

Introduction: "For how many soever be the promises of God, in him is the yea: wherefore also through him is the Amen, unto *the glory of God through us"*–II Cor. 1:20. "For all things are for your sakes, that the grace, being multiplied through the many, may cause the *thanksgiving to abound unto the glory of God."* I Cor. 4:15.

I. Temporal and spiritual blessings are promised to those *in Christ*–to those who faithfully serve Him. Rom. 8:28. This principle has always been true. Notice Deut. 7:11-8:20; 28th chapter; I Kings 8:35, 36, I Cor. 10:10, 11.

A. Many blessings are forfeited by God's children because they ask not or ask amiss. Jas. 4:3; I Jno. 5:14, 15.

B. James teaches that we should not plan to do anything, or expect to receive anything, it matters not how much natural law is involved or how many agencies are concerned, without recognizing that God is also involved and concerned. Jas. 4:13-17.

II. Some blessings for which we should give thanks unto the glory of God:
A. Ps. 1:1-3; Jas. 1:25.

B. Psa. 55:22; I Pet. 5:7.
C. Psa. 34:7; Heb. 1:14.
D. Psa. 37:25; Heb. 13:5; Matt. 6:25-34.
E. II Cor. 9:6-11.
F. Phil. 4:4-6.
G. Rom. 8:28, 32.
H. Rom. 5:1-10.
I. Rom. 8:17; Titus 2:11-14; 3:3-7.
J. Eph. 1:3.
K., Eph. 1:7; Heb. 8:12; I Jno. 1:9.
L. II Tim. 2:10.
M. Rom. 8:34.
N. Phil. 3:21.
O. I Jno. 5:11, II Pet. 1:11.
P. Col. 1:14.
Q. Rev. 14:13.

Conclusion: I Pet. 3:12; Rom. 4:20, 21. Therefore we can say with Paul, II Cor. 7:1; 4:15.

REVIEW QUESTIONS

1. Notice carefully the thought expressed in II Cor. 1:20 and II Cor. 4:15.
2. How much is included or how much is left out of "all things" in Romans 8:28?
3. From the Old Covenant, give examples of this principle. What does I Cor. 10:10, 11 teach?
4. Discuss Jas. 4:3, I Jno. 5:14, 15 and Jas. 4:13-17.
5. Are you truly thankful for the blessings listed? Do you give thanks for them? Name others not listed.
6. Read carefully I Pet. 3:12 and Rom. 4:20, 21.
7. Are you now ready to say with Paul, II Cor. 7:1; 4:15?

Lesson XIII

"GLORIFY GOD THEREFORE IN YOUR BODY"

Purpose: (1) To learn and appreciate the value of the human body;
(2) To encourage each one to use the body so as to be pleasing to God, therefore glorifying Him.

Introduction:

1. Three temples: (1) *Material temple* of Old Covenant where the Shechinah–glory (glory of Jehovah) dwelt, Ex. 29:42-46; (2) Another temple–*the body of Christ*–was consecrated as the dwelling place of our Savior, Jno. 2:19, 21; (3) Another temple–the residence and the shrine of the Spirit of God is within *each Christian,* I Cor. 3:16.

2. "Temple" used collectively, Eph. 2:21; and individually, I Cor. 6:19, 20.

I. The Christian Body:

A. *It is the Temple of the Holy Spirit.* I Cor. 6:19a. "The body is the framework of the sanctuary of the Divine Spirit. Like the temple of old, it is thus consecrated for a high, holy and sacred purpose. It is God's dwelling place. The little flower cup has the sun dwelling in it all the day, though it dwells in a thousand others; and its presence is made known by the color, fragrance, and growth of the flower." The same Spirit who abides in you, abides in every faithful member of the church, and this abiding is shown to others by the way you act and talk. I Jno., 4th Chapter. Notice particularly vss. 11-16.

B. *It is not our own,* I Cor. 6:19b. When we give Him our hearts, we should give Him our bodies also.

C. *It is for the Lord,* I Cor. 6:13c.
   1. For his service and glory, I Cor. 6:20.
   2. The Christian body is a member of Christ, I Cor. 6:15.
   3. Christ purchased our bodies, I Cor. 6:20a.

D. *It is cared for by God,* Matt. 6:25-33. (Notice also Ps. 41:1, 2 and Prov. 3:1-6). He feeds, clothes, shelters, guards and directs His children and makes all things work together for good, Rom. 8:28.

E. *It is to be raised,* I. Cor. 6:14, 15:35-58; Phil. 3:20, 21. Therefore we should think highly of our bodies, use them carefully and for His glory. I Cor. 6:20.

II. Injury: I Cor. 6:18; Gal. 5:19-21; I Pet. 2:1.
   A. How?
      1. Personal unholiness
      2. Unchristian spirit
      3. Conniving at unholiness in others
      4. Name others
   B. Results: I Cor. 3:17; Gal. 6:7, 8.

III. Conclusion: Gal. 6:9; I Pet. 2:5, 9; I Thess. 5:23; I Cor. 6:20.

REVIEW QUESTIONS

1. Name two temples in which God's spirit has dwelt. In what temple does He dwell today?

2. What evidence have we that God is dwelling in any particular person?

3. Discuss five reasons why we should take care of this body of ours?

4. How can personal unholiness injure one's body?

5. How does an unchristian spirit injure ones body?

6. How can tolerating these things in others injure MY body?

7. If we misuse the body, what may we expect as a result?

8. Read carefully each scripture listed in the conclusion.

Lesson XIV

FORGIVENESS

Purpose: (1) To warn against the dangers of nonforgiveness;
(2) To encourage each to acquire the forgiving attitude toward her fellowman, thereby pleasing God and glorifying Him.

Introduction: Few people pass through life without meeting with those who commit offenses against them—those who seek to damage their secular interest, their social enjoyment, or their moral reputation. How should one who wishes to glorify God act toward them? Examples: Lk. 23:34a; Acts 7:60; II Tim. 4:16.

I. Forgiveness, a divine command:

A. Eph. 4:31, 32; Col. 3:13 } forgive as God in Christ forgave you.
   1. God forgives abundantly; Isa. 55:7.
   2. God forgives fully, perfectly, and ungrudgingly, Heb. 10:16, 17; Psa. 103:10-12.
   3. God forgives cheerfully and generously as taught by the parable of the Prodigal Son, Lk. 15:11-32.

B. Always maintain a forgiving spirit, Lk. 17:3, 4; Matt. 18:21, 22.

II. Cost of nonforgiveness: By maintaining a nonforgiving spirit we shut out the possibility of:

A. God's forgiveness of our sins, Matt. 6:14, 15; Matt. 18:21-35.
B. Acceptable worship, Matt. 5:23, 24; Mk. 11:25.
C. True happiness, Lk. 11:28—an unrelenting bitterness against another never produces happiness.
D. Highest character, Rom. 8:9; Gal. 5:19-21; 22-26; Jas. 1:20.

Conclusion: If He who never wronged anyone and needed no forgiveness so freely forgives us, how much more ought we, who so frequently trespass both against Him and our fellow-man, to forgive those who trespass against us.

"Deal kindly with the erring
Oh! do not thou forget
However darkly stained by sin,
He is thy brother yet.

"Heir of the self-same heritage
Child of the self-same God
He hath but stumbled in the path
Thou hast in weakness trod.

"Deal kindly with the erring
Thou yet mayest lead him back
With Holy words and tones of love
From misery's erring track.

"Forget not thou hast often sinned
And sinful yet must be
Deal kindly with the erring one
As God has dealt with thee."

—Anonymous.

REVIEW QUESTIONS

1. Define forgiveness.

2. Give Christ's, Stephen's and Paul's attitudes toward those who had wronged them.

3. How much are Christians to forgive? How does God forgive?

4. What is the admonition in Lk. 17:3 and Matt. 18:21,22.

5. Discuss the cost of an unforgiving spirit. Can a child of God afford to let the day close without forgiving his fellowman? Why?

6. The amount under consideration in Matt. 18:21-35 is the ratio of ten million dollars to seventeen dollars. What is the application?

7. I Cor. 10:31b.

Lesson XV

THE MORE EXCELLENT WAY

Purpose: (1) To picture vividly the behavior of love;
(2) To encourage each to grow in the qualities of love that the life may be lived to the glory of God.

Introduction: Love should rule every thought and act. Notice I Pet. 4:8; I Jno. 2:5; I Jno. 4:7, 8, 12b, 20, 21; 5:2, 3; Rom. 13:9, 10; Jno. 14:15, 23, 24.

I. The *Love* that glorifies: I Cor. 13–See also Drummond, *The Greatest Thing in the World.*

A. Its necessity: contrasted with

1. *Eloquence,* I Cor. 13:1–all that a person has to say, even if it were the speech of angels, is nothing without love.
2. *Prophecy, Mysteries, Knowledge, Faith,* vs. 2–all that he may know is nothing without love.
3. *Charity, Sacrifice, Martrydom,* vs. 3–all that he can do is nothing without love.

What a man SAYS, what a man KNOWS, what a man DOES is without profit to himself unless he has the qualities of love.

II. The Qualities of Love: Vss. 4-13.

A. The behavior of love, vss. 4-7.

1. Love is *Patience,* vss. 4, 7–"Love Suffereth long"–calm, ready to work when needed in a meek and quiet spirit because love understands and waits. It tenaciously holds on even in adversities.
2. Love is *Kindness,* vs. 4–"And is kind"–an active

love is doing kind things for others, therefore letting our lights shine and thus glorifying God. We live this life only once, therefore use every opportunity to be kind.

3. Love is *Generosity,* vs 4–"Love envieth not." What is envy? "We need envy one thing and that is a large, rich, generous soul that envieth not."
4. Love is *Humility,* vs. 4–"Love vaunteth not itself, is not puffed up."–does not parade itself.
5. Love is *Courtesy,* vs. 5–"doth not behave itself unseemly." Manners make the measure of a man.
6. Love is *Unselfishness,* vs. 5–"seeketh not her own" –one who is happy in the happiness of others. There is no happiness in getting and having, but in giving.
7. Love is *Good-Tempered,* vs. 5–"is not easily provoked"–not easily ruffled, not a touchy disposition. Notice Matt. 18:6, 7.
8. Love is *Guilelessness,* vs. 5–"thinketh no evil"–sees the bright side, impugns no motives.
9. Love is *Sincerity,* vs. 6–"rejoiceth not in iniquity, but rejoiceth with the truth"–accepts only what is real, strives to get the facts, searches for truth with humble and unbiased mind and loves it, whatever he finds.

B. Permanence of love, vss. 8-13.

Conclusion:

A. How cultivate *Love?* Practice it. The world is not a playground but a schoolroom. The right attitude toward *cares, vexations,* will give you practice in love and therefore glorify God.
B. I Cor. 13:13–*Faith and Hope* are attributes of man only, but *Love* is also an attribute of God, therefore eternal. We must be like him, even toward our enemies, Matt. 5:43-48.
C. Notice what is to be included in the final judgment, Matt. 25:31-40.

REVIEW QUESTIONS

1. What is the significance of "above all things" in I Pet. 4:8. How can love fulfill the law?

2. Someone has said that I Cor. 13 breaks up love into its different elements as the prism breaks up the sun rays into its different colors. Explain.

3. Love is one of the incomparable things of Christianity, therefore to what is it contrasted? Explain how a person could have all these abilities and not have enough love to save him.

4. Study the nine elements which together make up love. Can you name a Biblical character and a person of your acquaintance who is outstanding in each of these characteristics?

5. In which do you need growth?

6. What lesson is taught in Matt. 5:43-48 and Matt. 25:31-40.

7. I Cor. 10:31b.

Lesson XVI

MY TONGUE

Purpose: (1) To warn against the dangers of the sins of the tongue;
(2) To encourage each to cultivate the speech that is becoming to a child of God and therefore glorify Him.

Introduction:

1. "The tongue is a little member," Jas. 3:5, and no man can tame it, 3:8; but it can be bridled, 1:26.
2. If not bridled, then it will defile the whole body, 3:5, 6.
3. If bridled, then Prov. 10:20; 15:4; 18:21; 21:23, and therefore the tongue can be made to glorify God.
4. The tongue compared to:
   (a) the horse's bridle, Jas: 3:3;
   (b) the ship's rudder, 3:4, and
   (c) a little fire, 3:5. Just as the spirited horse, the storm-tossed ship, and the raging fire can be brought under control, so can the tongue.

I. Sins of the tongue which must be brought under control:

A. Sins directly against God:
1. Blasphemy, Mk. 3:28-30.
2. Mockery of sacred things. Example: I Cor. 11:29.
3. Swearing, Jas. 5:12; Matt. 5:34-37; Matt. 23:20-22.

B. Sins against our fellowman:
1. Evil speaking: filthy and coarse jesting, harsh words said in anger, etc. Eph. 4:29; 5:4; Titus 3:1, 2; and Col. 3:8, 9.
2. Lying: exaggerations, conventional falsehoods in

business, false advertisements, Eph. 4:25; Rev. 21:8.

3. Slandering: backbiting, that which ruins the reputation of others, Psa. 101:5; Eph. 4:31.
4. Fault-finding, Rom. 14:13 (Moffat's translation); Matt. 7:1, 2: Jas. 4:11, 12.

C. Sins against ourselves: "Let loose the word, and you let loose the feelings." The bridling of the tongue means the bridling of the unruly passions of the heart. He who bridles not his tongue becomes immodest, indiscreet and intemperate. Notice Matt. 15:11.

"The Tongue is a Fire—and it is set on Fire of Hell!"

II. *The speech that glorifies:*

A. "Always with grace," Col. 4:6—courteous, dignified, wholesome, kind. Notice Prov. 31:26.

B. "Seasoned with salt"—healthful, interesting, pure. Notice Mk. 9:49, 50.
   1. Salt is seasoning; it gives pungency. The salted speech will keep. "The salt that seasons conversation often contains wholesome humor and wit."
   2. Salt is antiseptic: speech should have a positive purifying influence.

III. Conclusion:

A. Why watch the tongue? Psa. 15:1-3; Matt. 12:36, 37.
B. How can the tongue be bridled? By working at it and praying over it. Psa. 141:3; 19:14.

REVIEW QUESTIONS

1. Read Jas. 3:2.

2. How does James describe the tongue?

3. If the tongue is not bridled, what is the result? Explain. If it is bridled, what can be expected?

4. In what sense is the tongue like the "horse's bridle," the "ship's rudder" or "a little fire"?

5. Name the three classifications of the sins of the tongue.

6. Explain each of the sins directly against God. Can we blaspheme today? How? Is taking the Lord's Supper unworthily a mockery of sacred things? Do we have to use God's name before it could be called swearing? Take your by-words and analyze them. Are you swearing when you use them?

7. Study carefully the first three sins listed under "B." Are you guilty of any of these?

8. In what sense does the unbridled tongue cause us to sin against ourselves?

9. Describe the speech that is pleasing to God.

10. Why do we need to watch the tongue? What are idle words?

11. How are we to bridle the tongue?

12. I Cor. 10:31b.

Lesson XVII

THE CHRISTIAN'S TIME–REDEEM IT

Purpose: (1) To learn how to redeem time, and
(2) To show the importance of redeeming time.

Introduction: The Christian's time will be divided into two study lessons, namely, (1) redeeming the time, and (2) time spent in wholesome recreation. Notice the brevity of life as described in Jas. 4:14; Psa. 89:46, 47; 90:10-12. Someone has said, "Time is the most undefinable, yet paradoxical of things: the past is gone, the future is not come, and the present becomes the past even while we attempt to define it, and like the flash of lightning, at once exists and expires."

I. Redeeming the time: Eph. 5:15-21; Col. 4:5, 6.

A. Meaning of "redeeming the time": buying up opportunities and time; pay the price to make it your own to be used as needed.
Time can be bought or redeemed just as the farmer stores up "yesterday" in his barns; or as the student stores up knowledge and experiences gained from used opportunities. Later, as needed, the farmer can take things from his storehouse and the student can take up powers acquired by buying up time and use them to do the task before him.

II. How to redeem the time:
A. Eph. 5:15–"Walk circumspectly"–watch for the evil that might ensnare you as well as for opportunities to do good; WATCH the conduct.
B. Eph. 5:17–"Understand what the will of the Lord is" –STUDY. Notice II Tim. 2:15.
C. Eph. 5:18-20–"Be filled with the spirit"–WORSHIP.

D. Col. 4:5–"Walk in wisdom toward them that are without"–GOOD INFLUENCE. Notice II Cor. 3:2, 3.
E. Col. 4:6–"Speech seasoned with salt"–the pleasing wholesome speech that makes the Christian different from those of the world. BE GOOD!

III. Why redeem the time:

A. Eph. 5:15–"the days are evil."
B. Psa. 89:47–time is short.
C. James 4:14–time is uncertain.
D. Prov. 20:29–our strength uncertain. Youth and strength buying up time will not likely last to old age.
E. Matt. 12:36; Rom. 14:12–every moment to be accounted for.

Conclusion: "Buy up those moments which others seem to throw away; steadily improve every present moment, that you may in some measure regain the time you have lost. Let time be your chief commodity; deal in that alone; buy it all up, and use every portion of it yourself. Time is that on which eternity depends; in time you are to get a preparation for the kingdom of God; if you do not get this in time your ruin is inevitable; therefore buy up the time."–Adam Clarke. I Cor. 10:31–"Whatsoever ye do, do all to the glory of God."

REVIEW QUESTIONS

1. When did time begin? When will it end?

2. How much time can you really call your own? NOW is the time to prepare for eternity. Then how precious is time?

3. What is meant by redeeming time?

4. Explain how you may redeem time.

5. What reasons are given for redeeming time?

6. I Cor. 10:31b.

Lesson XVIII

THE CHRISTIAN'S TIME FOR RECREATION

Purpose: To learn some principles which will guide in selecting the right kind of recreation.

Introduction: Webster defines recreation as "the act of recreating; to give fresh life to." Therefore recreation is recreating the life that has been given in toil (either physical or mental) by some form of pastime or relaxation.

I. Some things Christians need to remember:

A. Phil. 1:27a–"Let your manner of life be worthy of the gospel."
B. Eph. 2:19; Phil. 3:20–We are citizens of a heavenly kingdom.
C. I Pet. 2:9–God's people are to "show forth the excellencies of Christ."

II. Some warnings:

A. I Jno. 2:15-17–"Love not the world–the world passeth away."
B. I Pet. 1:14, 15; Rom. 12:2–"Not fashioning yourselves to your former lusts–be holy in all manner of living."
C. Rom. 12:21–"Be not overcome with evil."
D. I Cor. 15:33–"Evil companionships corrupt good morals."

III. The Christian's recreational guide, then, should be:

A. What kind of fruits will it bear? Matt. 7:16-18.

B. What influence will it have upon me? On others? Notice I Cor. 8, 10; Matt. 18:7.

C. Not, may I do this, but ought I do this?

D. Not, is there any harm in this, but, is there any good in this?

E. Will it in fact RECREATE my life?

A favorable answer to these questions when applied to any form of pastime will make it a recreation suitable for a Christian.

Conclusion: Acts 17:31–The world is to be judged in *righteousness.* I Cor. 10:31–"Whatsoever ye do, do all to the glory of God."

REVIEW QUESTIONS

1. What does recreation mean?

2. Since the Bible does not tell how to act each minute of a twenty-four hour day, what are some abiding principles to guide a Christian in the use of our time?

3. What warnings have been given to Christians?

4. Select different forms of recreation peculiar to your community and to your age and apply the guiding questions to them. What is the result?

5. By what are we to be judged? Explain.

6. I Cor. 10:31b.

Lesson XIX

SOME THINGS CHRISTIANS MUST FOREGO

Purpose: To learn some basic Bible principles which will guide us in living the Christian life.

Introduction: The Christian is an epistle of Christ, therefore the world should be able to see the Christ-like spirit manifested in him. To glorify God, we must work together with Him to save ourselves and others. For this reason, there are several things a Christian must forego. Notice I Pet. 2:16; Gal. 5:13.

A Christian must forego:

I. Everything about which he has any doubt, Rom. 14:23. One who lacks faith in his actions is self condemned.

II. Everything that would be a stumbling block to a weak Christian, Rom. 14:13, 21; I Cor. 8:9, 12, 13. It is in the spirit of Christ, who "pleased not himself," Rom. 15:3, when one renounces some of his privileges in order that a stumbling block may be removed from a brother's path. Notice Mk. 9:42.

III. Everything that would place the Christian or the church in an unfavorable light, I Thess. 5:21, 22; II Cor. 8:20, 21. The Christian must forego all things connected with evil teaching or practice and those things which might bring reproach upon the church.

IV. Everything that would hinder our spiritual development and effective service. II Cor. 6:14-17. No kind of alliance should be made which hinders the living of a Christian life.

V. Everything upon which he cannot ask the blessing of God, Col. 3:17.

VI. Everything of which its character cannot be a glory to God. Matt. 5:16: I Peter 2:11, 12.

Conclusion: "Whatsoever ye do, do all to the glory of God." I Cor. 10:31.

REVIEW QUESTIONS

1. Even though the Christian is free from the bondage that governed the children of God under the Old Covenant is he compleetely free? What is freedom?

2. Should I do a thing that is right but which I believe to be wrong? May I do a thing that is wrong but I believe it to be right?

3. May I do a thing which would not do me any harm but might cause my associate to do wrong? Give examples. Notice I Cor. 8:7.

4. Give examples of point No. III in the outline.

5. Would some kind of business alliance come under the fourth point? Explain. What about some marriages? Name others.

6. Are your recreation, business, and marriage such that you can ask God to bless them as they are?

7. Read meditatively Matt. 5:16; I Pet. 2:11, 12; I Cor. 10:31.

Lesson XX

FINDING TRUE HAPPINESS

Purpose: To show the folly of temporary pleasure and happiness and to urge each to seek out those things which bring true happiness.

Introduction: "Life is too short for man with his limited abilities to search for true happiness without the experience of others. God has selected a man fully qualified to test all sources of worldly pleasures (and who writes a book—Ecclesiastes)—for our instruction."—E. N. Glenn.

I. Searching for happiness through

A. *Knowledge and wisdom,* Eccl. 1:12-18. Notice I Kings 3:9-28; 4:29-34. Result: Eccl. 1:17, 18. "With added experience and more minute examination, the wise man becomes more conscious of his own ignorance and impotence of the unsympathizing and uncontrollable course of nature, of the gigantic evils which he is powerless to remedy; this causes his sorrowful confession." (ver. 17b).

B. *Pleasure,* Eccl. 2:1-11. The effort to find happiness through pleasure was tried from three angles:

1. Sensuous enjoyment, vss. 1, 2. Compare I Kings 10:5, 11:1-3; I Tim. 5:6; Titus 3:3; Heb. 11:25; Jas. 5:5.
2. Revelry, vs. 3.
3. Culture and refinement, vss. 4-10; 12:9-12; I Kings 1:1-12. Solomon wrote about 3,000 proverbs, 1,005 songs. Result, Eccl. 2:11; 12:12.

   "The way of pleasure, however inviting, is not the way of safety or the way of peace. This passing happiness can lead to misery and shame."

C. *Wealth,* Eccl. 5:10-17; 6:1-6. Compare I Kings 4: 22-28; 10th chapter, 9:28. Result: Eccl. 5:10.

D. *Popular Religion,* Eccl. 5:1-7:irreverence, formality, insincerity, rash prayers, broken vows, disobedience. In the house of God where the above mentioned things are present, one cannot find a haven of refuge for the soul from vanity and care. Result: Eccl. 5:17.

E. Power and Honor, Eccl. 4:13-16. Compare I Kings 4:20, 21. Result: Eccl. 4:16.

"ALL IS VANITY AND VEXATION OF SPIRIT"

II. Lasting and true happiness, then, is found in Eccl. 12: 13, 14;

A. "Fear God": *reverence.*

B. "Keep His Commandments": *obedience.*

1. Reason:
   (a) "For this is the whole of man"–the source of true happiness.
   (b) "For God shall bring every work into judgment, with every secret thing, whether it be good, or whether it be evil"–the certainty of future judgment.

Conclusion: Matt. 16:26; I Cor. 10:31b.

REVIEW QUESTIONS

1. Ecclesiastes could be pictured as a play consisting of six scenes. Use this lesson as such:

Scene 1: Solomon, full of knowledge and wisdom.
- (a) What is the difference in knowledge and wisdom?
- (b) What is the result if one gives himself over to knowledge and wisdom? Can he be happy?

Scene 2: Solomon surrounded with ALL KINDS of pleasure.
- (a) Show how pleasure alone cannot give lasting happiness.
- (b) What was Solomon's conclusion?

Scene 3: Solomon surrounded with all the splendor that wealth could provide.
- (a) How wealthy was Solomon?
- (b) If wealth alone could bring happiness, do you think Solomon could have found it?
- (c) What was the conclusion?

Scene 4: Solomon surrounded with religious people (so-called) of the day.
- (a) Can happiness be found in a religious attitude that is insincere or one that consists of mere formality?
- (b) What was Solomon's conclusion?

Scene 5: Solomon surrounded with great power and honor.
- (a) How powerful was Solomon as King?
- (b) Did he find happiness in this? What was his conclusion?
- (c) Read Eccl. 7:1-8:17 as a general summary.

Scene 6: Solomon surrounded by vanishing plant and animal life—everything crumbling, Eccl. 12.
- (a) Where is lasting and true happiness to be found?
- (b) Give several reasons why this is true.

2. Memorize Matt. 16:26.

3. I Cor. 10:31b.

Lesson XXI

BUILDING A CHRISTIAN CHARACTER AND REPUTATION

Purpose: To learn what makes a Christian character and how to acquire it; to urge each to build toward the goal.

Introduction: What people think of you (reputation) is based upon what you are (character). "The influence of Christian character on the world is incalculable. By unbecoming conduct we may harden men in sin and unbelief; by becoming conduct we may prepare the way of the Lord." Notice I Pet. 2:11, 12.

I. Description of a Christian character:

A. A meek and quiet spirit, I Pet. 3:3, 4. Times and conditions may change the outward appearance of everyone but the "meek and quiet spirit" remains unchanged with changing time. Christian character grows from within.

B. II Pet. 1:5-7: Here are listed seven graces which supplement each other. No one can be omitted without weakening the rest. One grace apart from the others could be disastrous. Faith is already present. Faith is the primary essential of the whole character. Only from faith can the graces spring. Notice Heb. 11:6.

1. *Virtue*—manly courage or moral energy. To our faith must be supplied the courage to act—not passively believe but actively live. Notice Matt. 7:21.
2. *Knowledge*—enlightened judgment. Faith and energy without knowledge would be a dangerous

zeal. Notice Rom.: 10:1-4.

3. *Temperance*–self control. This grace must be added (supplied in) to virtue and knowledge so that bodily appetites, desires, tempers, etc. might be brought into subjection. Without it there is no unity of purpose. Notice I Cor. 9:25-27.
4. *Patience*–patient endurance. If a person stops short of this–adds only the first three–there would be "rigorism." He who would practice self control will need patience to endure difficulties. Notice Rom. 5:3.
5. *Godliness*–a spirit of reverence, a God-fearing disposition. The first four graces alone would mean "Stoicism." The godly person sets God always before him; his effort is to live unto the Lord, to seek His glory. His reverence for God controls his whole life, therefore this link cannot be left out of the chain of graces. Notice I Tim. 4:8.
6. *Brotherly kindness*–love of the brethren. To have only the first five graces would be selfish. We are taught this grace also in I Jno. 4:20, 21; 5:1.
7. *Charity*–love. The first six graces would also be selfish. We are to show our love and concern for all mankind for whom Christ died.

II. How to attain this kind of character:

A. Adorn yourselves; I Pet. 3:3.
B. Giving diligence–add (supply in), II Pet. 1:5.
C. Study of and association with models, especially Christ, I Pet. 3;5; Acts 4:13.

III. Reasons for acquiring the Christian character:

A. Better knowledge of Christ, II Pet. 1:8.
B. An obligation to Christ for pardoning of past sins, II Pet.: 1:9.
C. The graces are the only ground upon which Christians are assured entrance into heaven, II Pet. 1:10, 11.
D. This kind of character will have a good reputation,

Prov. 22:1; 23:7a.

E. The proper response of love and faith.

Conclusion: Phil. 4:8; I Cor. 5:12; I Cor. 10:31.

REVIEW QUESTIONS

1. Try to describe the influence of Christian character. What would your community, your social group, your political group be without it? Can you imagine a Christless world—a world without any Christian character to influence every activity of life?

2. From whence comes a Christian character? Explain.

3. What is essential to the building of a Christian character? Why?

4. Show how each grace is dependent upon the succeeding one.

5. How may a person obtain this kind of character? Explain each way.

6. Why should a person acquire this kind of character?

7. Read carefully the scriptures listed in the conclusion.

Lesson XXII

SPIRITUAL ATHLETICS

Purpose: To encourage all to strive lawfully for the crown so that their labors will not have been in vain.

Introduction: The Christian life has been compared to a foot-race and to a boxing contest, games which are familiar to all people. It is similar to these in that it is an intense activity of short duration in which certain rules must be observed in order to enter and win.

I. Grecian Games.

A. Conditions of entering the games: "For thirty days previous to the conflict the candidates had to attend the exercises of the gymnasium, and only after the fulfillment of these conditions were they allowed, when the time arrived, to contend in the sight of assembled Greece."

B. The runner or fighter cannot run or fight anywhere but must be a lawful contestant in the event marked out for him.

II. Spiritual Athletics–The Christian Race.

A. Prepare for the race by lawfully entering the course that "is set before you," II Tim. 2:5; Heb. 11:6; Lk. 13:3; Matt. 10:32; Gal. 3:26, 27.

B. Conditions of success in the race:

1. "Lay aside every weight," Heb. 12:1–cast off everything that encumbers. This includes every weight of cares, of interests, of attachments, of relationships, etc., that are not favorable to advancement in the race. It also includes all things

which in themselves are innocent but which wrap themselves tightly around our hearts so as to impede our progress. Example: Love of comfort, luxury and other indulgences.

2. Lay aside the sin of unbelief so you can "press on to the goal." Notice Phil. 3:13, 14.
3. "Run with patience," Heb. 12:1–Steadfastness. Cf. Gal. 6:9; II Thess. 3:13; Matt. 10:22b. Notice Abraham as an example. Heb. 6:13-15.
4. "Exercise self-control in all things," I Cor. 9:25a. This "applies to all the passions of the body, indulgences of the appetite, and the relationships of life. The Christian is called to be temperate alike in all his thoughts, emotions, words and ways; in his joys and sorrows, his schemes and activities, his personal indulgences and personal mortifications; and in his worldly ambitions."
5. Self-discipline, I Cor. 9:27. "The body is the temple of the Holy Spirit, and therefore it should be made the submissive servant of the soul's diviner purposes when it dares to obstruct the spirit in its path to the heavenly crown."

III. The Winner:

A. He who contends lawfully, II Tim. 2:5.
B. He who finishes the race, II Tim. 4:7.

IV. The Reward:

A. An incorruptible crown, I Cor. 9:25 }
B. Crown of righteousness, II Tim. 4:7, 8 } Eternal life

Conclusion: Heb. 12:1-4; I Cor. 10:31b.

REVIEW QUESTIONS

1. Give a brief account of the contestant's activities in the Grecian games.

2. How does a person become eligible to enter the Christian race? Have you entered the course that "is set before you"?

3. Discuss and explain the five things necessary to win the crown in the Christian race.

4. In the Grecian game, only he who lawfully finished first was crowned. In what way does this differ in spiritual athletics? Who is the winner?

5. What is the reward of those who lawfully enter and faithfully finish the Christian race? Can anyone afford to miss this reward?

6. What is the thought in Heb. 12:1-4?

7. I Cor. 10:31b.

Lesson XXIII

MAKING A LIVING

Purpose: To show that useful work is a Christian duty.

Introduction: "It was the purpose of God from the beginning for man to work. God gave man hands, brawn, and muscles. He gave him a mind, with intellectual powers. The possession of these things emphasizes the fact that he should use them. To use them is to work."—Elam's Notes.

I. Work commanded: Gen. 3:19; Ex. 20:9; II Thess. 3:10; I Thess. 4:11.

II. Motives for work:

A. To support self and family, Acts 20:34, 35; I Tim. 5:8.
B. To give to the helpless, Acts 20:34, 35; Eph. 4:28; Jas. 1:27.
C. Support the gospel, Mk. 16:15, 16; I Cor. 9:13, 14; I Tim. 5:17, 18.

III. Wrong methods of getting money, Amos 5:11-13; Jer. 17:9-11; Jas. 5:4-6; I Cor. 6:10; Prov. 11:1.

A. Anything that afflicts or oppresses the poor.
B. Bribery.
C. No extortioner; no stealing.
D. No cheating.
E. Anything that is harmful.

IV. Various thoughts concerning work:

A. God approves:
   1. Economy and thrift, Prov. 10:4, 5.

2. Industry, Prov. 12:11; 21:5; 12:24; 13:4.
3. Honesty, Prov. 12:22.
4. Justice, Jas. 5:4.
5. Diligence, Rom. 12:11; Eccl. 9:10.

B. A warning, Prov. 24:30-34.

C. Woman, helper, Prov. 31.

Conclusion: "Slothful Christians are no more pleasing to God than lazy servants are to their masters. Both disgrace their professions. We should be reminded that since work is so important for our physical, moral, and spiritual welfare, God would direct us in doing the right kind of work. We should seek to know the kind of work that God wants us to do and do that. (Phil. 4:4-6). Everyone should have an honest occupation. This occupation should be followed diligently and honestly." I Cor. 10:31.

REVIEW QUESTIONS

1. Was man told to work before any curse was placed upon mankind? Gen. 2:15. Is work or idleness a curse?

2. What should be a Christian's motive in working? Name other motives which some people, who take no thought of God's plan, have for working.

3. May a Christian engage in any kind of work? Why? Select several different occupations and test them according to God's principles.

4. Meditate upon the various thoughts concerning work. If the homemaker is not doing public work, does she have a place in this lesson? How?

5. What principle covers all work, whether it be husband, wife, or children?

Lesson XXIV

CHRISTIAN EMPLOYER AND EMPLOYEE

Purpose: To learn the principles governing Christian employers and employees in business and to encourage them to practice the principles set forth in the Scriptures that God may be glorified.

Introduction: We do not have masters and servants today but we do have, and always will have, some who command or boss and some who obey or work under a boss—the employer and employee. The PRINCIPLES laid down in the Bible for master and servant are those that should be exercised by the employer and employee.

I. Employee, Eph. 6:5-8; Col. 3:22-25; I Tim. 6:12; Titus 2:9, 10.

  A. Duty: Obedience. The disobedient employee commits a double sin because (1) he is unfaithful to his contract, and (2) he robs his employer of unearned wages.

  B. Quality of service
    1. Sincere—"in singleness of heart."
    2. Earnest—"work heartily."
    3. Thorough—"not with eye-service as men-pleasers, but as servants of Christ."
    4. Cheerful—"with good will."

The employer cannot see all your work all the time but GOD CAN, therefore the work should not be the kind that cannot bear testing nor should you do good work only when the employer is watching. Dishonest work should be avoided as much as dishonest words. The wrongs done by an employer do not justify wrong doing by the employee. Study I Pet. 2: 18-25; I Kings 18:3, 4; Gen. 39: 3, 6, 22, 23. The Christian employee desires to do his duty because he is serving God as well as man.

C. Principle:
   1. "As unto Christ and not unto men."
   2. "Fearing the Lord." Notice I Sam. 16:7; Neh. 5:15.
   3. "Doing the will of God from the heart."

D. Reward: Eph. 6:8; Col. 3:24; I Tim. 6:1; Titus 2:9, 10.

E. Warning: Col. 3:25.

II. Employer, Eph. 6:9; Col. 4:1:
   A. Duty:
      1. Justice } "render that which is just and equal"
      2. Equity }
      3. Practice the Golden rule, Matt. 7:12–"Do the same things unto them."

III. Motives for true service to employer and employee; but sustain a common relationship to Christ:
   A. Both are his servants, Eph. 6:9; Col. 3:24b; 4:1b. Both must give an account.
   B. All work is done in God's sight as service to Christ.
   C. All ministering may be done to God's glory for there is no respecter of persons, I Pet. 4:11b.
   D. Christ will rightly give out retribution and reward, Eph. 6:8, Col. 3:24.

Conclusion: Our genuineness of life shows itself in our daily work as well as in worship. Adopt the motto of "He profits most who serves best." I Cor. 10:31–"Whatsoever ye do, do all to the glory of God."

REVIEW QUESTIONS

1. What does the employee owe the employer? Discuss each thing listed.

2. What is taught in I Pet. 2:18-25; I Kings 18:3, 4; Gen. 39:3, 6, 22, 23?

3. What is the Christian's higher motive for faithful service to his employer? What will be his reward? What warning is given?

4. What does the employer owe the employee?

5. What do the employer and employee have in common?

6. Do you agree with the motto suggested in the conclusion? Why?

7. I Cor. 10:31b.

Lesson XXV

CITIZENSHIP

Purpose: To learn the Christian's attitude toward and obligations to the civil government.

Introduction: Normal intelligent people are responsible for their conduct. There must be rules or laws for the regulation of human conduct. Laws impose both duties and prohibitions. Both are binding. A Christian should not violate a faulty law but should work to have it repealed. The respect for constituted authority—at home, at school, in the nation, and in spiritual matters—needs to be emphasized and practiced by all. The principles govern all relations and interests of the Christian, therefore his relation to civil authorities is explained.

I. The Purpose of Civil Government:

A. Rom. 13:4; I Pet. 2:14, 15; to preserve order; to restrain evil doers; to protect the innocent; to be a "terror" to evil doers; to be an "avenger for wrath"; to be God's servant for good to the law-abiding; to punish wrong doers.

II. Christian's Duty Toward Civil Government:

A. Subjection. Rom. 13:1; I Pet. 2:13.
   1. When laws are made, respect them.
   2. When taxes are levied, pay them.
   3. When service is required, render it.
   4. Obedience limited, Acts 4:19, 20; 5:29.

B. "Honor the king," I Pet. 2:17.

C. Pray for civil authorities, I Tim. 2:1-4.

III. Christian's Motives in Obeying Civil Governments:

A. For the Lord's sake, I Pet. 2:13.

B. It is the will of God, I Pet. 2:15; Rom. 13:2.

C. For conscience sake, Rom. 13:5.

D. True patriotism of an individual is righteousness, Prov. 14:34.

Conclusion: A bad citizen cannot be a good Christian. Government would be easy if everyone were a Christian who realized his duties as a citizen. I Cor. 10:31b.

REVIEW QUESTIONS

1. Why is civil government a necessity?

2. What is the Christian's duty toward the civil government? Discuss each.

3. Most people obey civil government because they have to do it. What is the Christian's motive? Discuss.

4. What is true patriotism? Can you give examples in Old Covenant where a city or nation suffered because of its unrighteous people? What lesson may we today draw from this principle?

5. I Cor. 10:31b.

Lesson XXVI

MAKING THE HOME CHRISTIAN

Purpose: To impress deeply the scriptural teachings concerning the relationships and duties of the members of a Christian household.

Introduction: "As the kind of seed sown determines the kind of plant, and the principle involved regulates the practice, so the kind of homes in which people are reared does much in shaping their destiny in whatever association they may be.–The home must furnish the material to become members of the church."–Elam's Notes.

I. *The Marriage Relation,* Eph. 5:22-33; Col. 3:18, 19; I Pet. 3:1-7; I Cor. 7:39; Matt. 19:9; Rom. 7:2, 3; I Cor. 7:10-15.

  A. "Wives, be in subjection to your own husbands–as the church is subject to Christ."
     "Let the wife see that she treats her husband with respect."
  B. "The husband is the head of the wife as Christ is head of the church," "Husbands, love your wives, even as Christ also loved the church"–"Love their own wives as their own bodies."
  C. Second marriage after death of the husband is "only in the Lord."
  D. Fornication is the only cause of divorce.

II. *The Parent-Child Relation,* Eph. 6:4; Col. 3:21; Heb. 12:5-8; II Cor. 12:14; Titus 2:4.

  A. Provoke not.

  B. Nurture them.

C. Teach them.

D. Discipline them.

E. Provide for them.

F. Love them.

III. *The Child-Parent Relation,* Eph. 6:1-3; Col. 3:20; Prov. 6:20-23; I Tim. 5:4.

A. Obey your parents in the Lord.

B. Honor thy father and mother.

C. Requite parents–repay or show gratitude.

Conclusion: The more Christian homes we make, the better our nation will be. The church of our Lord will prosper when more homes are based upon Christian principles. Let us do our part in making the home Christian. I Cor. 10:31b.

REVIEW QUESTIONS

1. How and to what extent do homes affect the country? The church?

2. What place does the wife hold in the marriage relation? How is the church subject to Christ? Evaluate these statements: (1) "Christ needs a body upon earth; the body needs a head in heaven, therefore dependent upon each other; as are husband and wife." (2) "Man rules the woman he weds as love rules." (3) "Man is the head provider, woman is the helper; therefore, they are co-laborers." (4) "The wife's subjection is no more exacting than man's obligation." (5) "Divorce is as tragic as the separation of the church from Christ."

3. What restriction is laid upon a second marriage?

4. What is the only ground for divorce?

5. What obligations do parents owe their children? What is the duty of the child toward his parent?

6. I Cor. 10:31b.

Lesson XXVII

TRIAL OF YOUR FAITH

Purpose: To learn the Christian's attitude toward trials and to urge all to accept the encouragement offered in the Scriptures.

Introduction: "Yea, and all that would live godly in Christ Jesus shall suffer persecution," II Tim. 3:12. *"Beloved think it not strange* concerning the fiery trial among you, which cometh upon you," I Pet. 4:12. *"—through many tribulations* we must enter into the Kingdom of God." Acts 14:22.

I. The Trials—The Testing is:

A. Temporary—"for a little while," I Pet. 1:6, 7.
B. Painful—"put to grief in manifold trials."

II. Purpose of Testing: Necessary—"if need be," I Pet. 1:6.

A. To try the genuineness of it—"the proof of your faith," I Pet. 1:7; Jas. 1:3. Just as the chaff looks like wheat but is not, so the seemliness of conduct especially at worship, may look like faith, and yet faith may be absent.
B. To purify, I Pet. 1:7; Heb. 12:5-11 (especially verses 10 and 11). Notice Job 23:10, 11.
C. To develop patience, Jas. 1:3.
D. To train for The Life Eternal—"May be found unto praise and glory and honor at the revelation of Jesus Christ," I Pet. 1:7; "that ye may be perfect and entire, lacking in nothing," Jas. 1:3, 4.

III. Nature of the Testing, Matt. 5:10-12:

A. "Reproach you."

B. "Persecute you."
C. "Say all manner of evil against you falsely, for my sake."
D. Poverty?
E. Unpopularity?
F. Contempt?
G. Business?
H. Intellectual?
I. Sorrow?

IV. Attitude of the Christian Toward These Trials, Matt. 5:12; Jas. 1:2; I Pet. 4:13, 19.

V. Reward for those that "hath been approved," I Pet. 4:14; Jas. 1:12; Matt. 5:10, 12; I Pet. 5:10; Jas. 1:2.

A. "Blessed."
B. "Strengthen you."
C. "The Spirit of glory and the Spirit of God resteth upon you."
D. "Theirs is the kingdom of heaven."
E. "Great is your reward in heaven."
F. "Receive the crown of life." Cf. Matt. 5:11, 12; Jno. 17:3; 14:21, 23; Rom. 8:17; II Cor. 4:17.

Conclusion: I Pet. 4:14-19; Rom. 8:28; I Cor. 10:31—"Whatsoever ye do, do all to the glory of God."

REVIEW QUESTIONS

1. How do you know the strength of any material? Make the application to children of God.

2. Why do you test a thing which you intend to use for a special thing? (Make the application.)

3. Can you recall that God ever exalted anybody before testing him? Consider Adam's and Eve's testing? Abraham's testing? Joseph's testing? Moses' testing? Christ's testing?

4. Describe the testing spoken of in I Pet. 1:6, 7.

5. Discuss God's reasons for testing children.

6. Name many ways a person can be tested. Which ones have you experienced? Did you stand the test?

7. What is the Christian's attitude toward these trials?

8. If the testing is endured what promise awaits the individual?

9. Read carefully each scripture listed in the conclusion.

Lesson XXVIII

OVER-ANXIETY

Purpose: To impress upon each one the privilege of relying upon God so that Phil. 4:4-6 can be obeyed.

Introduction: Meaning of:

1. Anxious–distracting care, harassing care.
2. Prayer–the converse with God.
3. Supplication–the direct petitions for ourselves and others.
4. Thanksgiving–the accompaniment of prayer.

I. The Wise Counsel of the Apostle–"In nothing be anxious."

A. Negative meaning: (1) not indolent improvidence (II Thess. 3:10); not reckless carelessness (Matt. 25: 14-30); not cares about health or getting a livelihood (I Tim. 5:8); not cares about those who are near and dear to us (Eph. 6:4); not cares about the welfare of the church (II Cor. 11:28).

B. Positive meaning: We are not to be harassed by cares: not over-anxious so that we distract our thoughts from the service of God and are hindered in our growth in holiness. Notice I Pet. 5:7; Rom. 8:28; Matt. 6:33, 34.

C. Reasons for not being over-anxious:
   1. Our anxiety will not ward off the anticipated evil.
   2. The evil may turn out for our good.
   3. It is a disregard of a divine command.
   4. It is a distrust of God's power and wisdom.
   5. It doubts the reality of the promises of God.
   6. It deters from duty.
   7. It spoils the temper and comfort of work.
   8. It hinders spiritual energy.

II. The Remedy: "In everything by prayer and supplication with thanksgiving let your requests be made known unto God."

A. Christ taught the way to conquer earthly anxiety:
   1. Trust in the Father, Matt. 6:32.
   2. Transfer our care to a more noble object, Matt. 6:33.

B. Divine remedy according to Paul:
   1. Prayer–Be anxious about nothing by making supplication about everything, "Be careful for nothing; be prayerful for everything; be thankful for anything."
   2. Thanksgiving–Grateful recollections of the past will greatly allay anxiety about the future.

III. The Result: "And the peace of God, which passeth all understanding, shall guard your hearts and your thoughts."

A. God answers the prayer of anxiety with a gift of peace.
B. The hearts and thoughts will be guarded.

IV. The abiding source: "In Christ Jesus."

Conclusion: I Cor. 10:31b.

REVIEW QUESTIONS

1. Memorize Phil. 4:4-6.
2. Explain the terms: anxious, prayer, supplication, thanksgiving.
3. Explain the difference in having cares and being harassed by cares.
4. Discuss the reasons for not being over-anxious. Name others not listed in this outline.
5. What is the remedy? What comfort is in this remedy?
6. What results are we promised? Do you really believe it?
7. Evaluate the expression that this peace is "in Christ Jesus."

Lesson XXIX

CONTENTMENT

Purpose: To encourage each to be content, in the Bible sense, which is one prerequisite of happiness.

Introduction: Contentment, in a Bible sense, is not the contentment of indifference, of indolence, or unambitious stupidity, but the contentment of industrious fidelity. Notice I Tim. 6:8; 6:6; Phil. 4:11-13.

I. The duty, Heb. 13:5, 6; I Tim. 6:6.

II. The basis for encouraging one to fulfill this duty, Heb. 13:5c. Notice Deut. 31:6; Joshua 1:5; I Chron. 28:20; Matt. 28:20b; Heb. 13:5c.

A. The abiding presence of God with us guarantees the supply of all our needs, Phil. 4:19.
  1. *Provisions,* Psa. 84:11; Rom. 8:32; Matt. 6:25-34.
  2. *Protection,* Psa. 121; Rom. 8:31; I Pet. 3:13, 14; Matt. 10:28-31.
  3. *Guidance,* Psa. 48:14; 73:23, 24; Prov. 3:56; Psa. 25, 9, 10; Rom. 8:28.

III. A triumphant assurance, Phil. 4:6; Psa. 118:6.

A. Man's need of help, Acts 17:25, 28.
B. God's provisions for help:
  1. Gal. 6:2–helping each other. Notice Psa. 37:25.
  2. Heb. 4:15, 16; Matt. 21:22; Jno. 15:7, 16-23, 24; I Jno. 5:14, 15–prayer.
C. The assurance of God's help is based upon His promise, Phil. 4:5c, 6. Notice Num. 23:19; Matt. 24:35; Jno. 10:35; II Tim. 2:13. God's help is all sufficient, ever

available and ever gracious.

D. This confidence inspires the courage of the believer, therefore produces contentment, Phil. 4:6. Notice Rom. 8:31, 32, 38, 39; I Pet. 3:12-14; Psa. 23; 46:1-3.

Conclusion: I Cor. 10:31b.

REVIEW QUESTIONS

1. Memorize Heb. 13:5, 6 and I Tim. 6:6.

2. Quote scripture showing that God is ever present with His children.

3. What has been promised to faithful followers of God?

4. How does God provide for man's real needs?

5. What assurance have we that God is able and willing to help?

6. How, then, does contentment come to a child of God?

7. How does I Cor. 10:31b fit into this lesson?

Lesson XXX

DO ALL TO THE GLORY OF GOD

I Cor. 10:31

Purpose: (1) To encourage each Christian to walk circumspectly and,
(2) To live so that the life will be a Glory to God.

Introduction: We glorify God by so living that His life shines out through our conduct. Gospel preaching and teaching MUST be supported by gospel living. The world can see a sermon when it will not go to hear one.
Whatsoever Ye Do, Do All To The Glory of God because a Christian is:

I. The *Light* of the world, Matt. 5:14-16. Christians reflect the true light, Jno. 8:12. Notice Phil. 2:14-16. The light streams out by good works.

II. The *Salt* of the earth, Matt. 5:13. Salt purifies and preserves. It will prevent corruption, but it will not cure it. The people of the Covenant were the people of salt, Num. 18:19. Sodom was destroyed because it did not have enough righteous (salt) people in it. Gen. 18:22-19:25. Notice Prov. 14:34. If you wish to be truly patriotic, be righteous.

III. An *Epistle* of Christ, II Cor. 3:2, 3. All men, seeing your transformed lives should read you as an epistle of which Christ is the author and dictator, and you are the earthly penman.

IV. *Kingdom of Priests* unto God, a *Royal Priesthood,* Rev. 1:6; I Pet. 2:9. This is the highest attainment among men, therefore picturing the exalted state of the Children of God. Christians are to exhibit a holy and useful life after the pattern of their King and High Priest, the Lord Jesus Christ.

V. *Children, heirs,* Gal. 3:26; Rom. 8:16, 17; I Jno. 3:2; Col. 3:4. Christians should live so as to honor the name they wear–glorify Him. I Pet. 4:16.

Conclusion: Let each examine herself and strive earnestly to live so that God will be glorified.

REVIEW QUESTIONS

1. What are the peculiar characteristics of light? Apply these to the Christian.
2. What are the characteristics of salt? Apply these to the Christian.
3. Show how the Christian is an epistle of Christ.
4. Evaluate the expression that Christians are a "Kingdom of priests, a royal priesthood."
5. Of what significance is it that Christians are children and heirs of God?
6. I Cor. 10:31.

Lesson XXXI

OUR ETERNAL HOME

Purpose: To encourage each to be faithful unto death so that the eternal home will be with the glorified; and, to explain the Bible teaching on the life after death.

Introduction: This lesson is the story of a rich man who had the mammon of unrighteousness in abundance. Because he failed to live so as to be pleasing to God—to GLORIFY HIM—he found himself, after death, without a friend and excluded from the habitation of Lazarus, who was pleasing to the Father.

I. The Rich Man and Lazarus, Lk. 16:19-31.

A. A series of contrasts:
   1. Home life before death, vss. 19-21.
   2. Death and burial, vs. 22.
   3. Home life after death, vs. 23.

B. Lessons: *Death will bring the just reward,* vss. 24-31.

II. Lesons suggested:

A. The sin of the rich man was not in having riches but in his attitude toward and his use of the riches.

B. Righteousness of the poor man was not in his being poor but because his life was pleasing to God—glorify Him.

C. Now is the time to prepare for life after death.

D. The word of God is a sufficient guide to follow in preparing for heaven.

E. Life after death:
   1. Death means a separation and an end of a state or condition. Notice Rom. 7:9; Col. 3:3; I Tim. 5:6;

Gen. 35:18; I Kings 17:21, 22; Eccl. 12:7; Lk. 23:43, 46; Acts 7:59.

2. Separation of body and spirit:
   (a) Hades (Greek) or Sheol (Hebrew) unseen world.
   (b) Tartarus (Greek)–prison house, II Pet. 2:4.
   (c) Paradise (Persian)–pleasure garden, Lk. 23:43.
   (d) Great Gulf, Lk. 16:26.
   (e) Judgment, Heaven, Gehenna, Rev. 20:11-15.

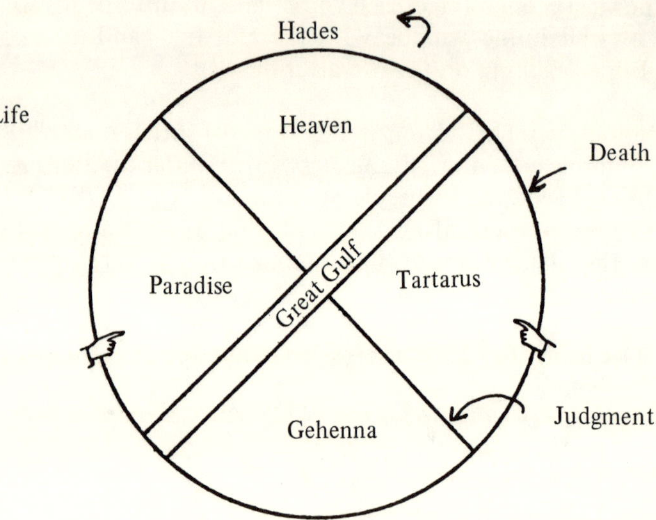

3. New Testament teaching concerning departed spirits:
   (a) Acts 2:34, "David ascended not into the heavens."
   (b) Lk. 23:43, "Today thou shalt be with me in paradise–" Jno. 20:17, "Not yet ascended to the Father."
   (c) Lk. 16:19:31–The rich man was in Tartarus; the poor man in Paradise or Abraham's bosom.
   (d) The final judgment, Matt. 25:31-34; 12:41, 42; II Cor. 5:10; Jude 6; II Pet. 2:9; II Tim. 4:1; Rev. 20:13. Rewards and condemnation come at the final judgment. Luke 14:14; Jno. 14:1-3; II Tim. 4:7, 8; II Cor. 5:10.

Conclusion: A. Jno. 8:31, 32; Rev. 2:10d.
B. Heaven and Gehenna are forever, Rev. 20:10; Matt. 25:31, 32, 46.

REVIEW QUESTIONS

1. Describe the lives of the rich man and Lazarus before and after death.

2. At what time were they on an equal?

3. What is the lesson of this incident? Evaluate it.

4. Discuss A, B, C, and D under "II."

5. Show from Bible references what death means.

6. After death, where is the spirit of the one who spends his life here glorifying God? Of the one who leaves God out of his life? Describe these places.

7. If the home after death is decided at death, why a final judgment?

8. How long is ETERNAL life and ETERNAL condemnation?

9. Quote Jno. 8:31, 32 and Rev. 2:10.

10. Quote I Cor. 10:31 and give in your own words what it means to you.